SHIPWRECKS
OF THE
SOLENT

RICHARD M. JONES

AMBERLEY

For Alexander McKee
A man who did so much for maritime history

Also by Richard M. Jones:

The Great Gale of 1871

Lockington: Crash at the Crossing

Capsized in the Solent: The SRN6-012 Disaster

End of the Line: The Moorgate Disaster

Collision in the Night: The Sinking of HMS Duchess

Royal Victoria Rooms: The Rise and Fall of a Bridlington Landmark

RMS Titanic: The Bridlington Connections

The 50 Greatest Shipwrecks

Britain's Lost Tragedies Uncovered

The Burton Agnes Disaster

When Tankers Collide: The Pacific Glory Disaster

The Diary of a Royal Marine: The Life and Times of George Cutcher

The Farsley Murders

Living the Dream, Serving the Queen

Around the World in Shipwreck Adventures

Boleyn Gold (Fiction)

Austen Secret (Fiction)

Gunpowder Wreck (Fiction)

Cretil the Cat (Children's book)

Lost at Sea in Mysterious Circumstances

A–Z of Bridlington

First published 2024

Amberley Publishing
The Hill, Stroud
Gloucestershire, GL5 4EP

www.amberley-books.com

ISBN 978 1 3981 1750 1 (print)
ISBN 978 1 3981 1751 8 (ebook)

British Library Cataloguing in Publication Data.
A catalogue record for this book is available from the British Library.

Typesetting by SJmagic DESIGN SERVICES, India.
Printed in Great Britain.

Contents

Introduction

From an early age I had always been fascinated by shipwrecks, the stories of ships like *Titanic* and *Bismarck* providing hours of reading, leading to many more hours trawling through libraries and archives before finally going on to writing my own books on some of the more forgotten wrecks.

So when I was asked to write about shipwrecks in the Solent I jumped at the chance. The Solent is the body of water that separates the southern English coast from the Isle of Wight, a very busy shipping region with two major ports in a very small area – Portsmouth and Southampton.

With the Royal Navy warships, cargo ships, ferries and a few liners transiting Portsmouth and the larger cruise liners and container ships going up to Southampton, it would be inevitable that over time one or two of them would come to grief here. Add two world wars into the equation and you have a seabed littered with ships, each one telling a story of our maritime past.

As there are so many shipwrecks in the Solent it is hard to document them all in one book, so I have chosen a variety of stories starting in the 1400s with the *Grace Dieu*, through to the more famous wrecks like the *Mary Rose* and *Royal George*, all the way up to the headline-hitting *Hoegh Osaka*, which would have joined the others on the seabed if it wasn't for the skill of the salvage workers to get it back into port.

Another fact to note is the Royal Navy prefix HMS, for His/Her Majesty's Ship. The title 'His Majesty's Ship' was used from the reign of King Charles II after the official forming of the Royal Navy, but the first recording of it being abbreviated to HMS was in 1789 for HMS *Phoenix*, although in the case of the shipwrecks in this book after the mid-1700s, they will be prefixed as such.

Previously I have written books on some of the wrecks featured here. *Capsized in the Solent* told the story of the *SRN6-012* hovercraft disaster, *When Tankers Collide* was about the *Pacific Glory, Britain's Lost Tragedies Uncovered* had a chapter on the *Flag Theofano* and two of my generic shipwreck books contained the *Mary Rose*. But this book contains new information that I have gained since those were published and it is my pleasure to be able to update their story with new insight from *Mary Rose* divers, a survivor's story from the hovercraft and memorial plaques that have since been placed to remember the *Flag Theofano* and *Pacific Glory* disasters. These additions to the stories of these ships mean that the chapters on those wrecks in this particular book are in fact never-before-published details and photographs.

Each wreck has a unique insight into the history of this area, consisting of cargo ships, warships, submarines and even a hovercraft. Some wrecks were salvaged; some are still on the seabed today. Every one of them deserves their story telling.

LOSS OF THE "ROYAL GEORGE," AT SPITHEAD.

1871 image titled 'Loss of the Royal George at Spithead'.

1
Grace Dieu

The port of Southampton has been a hive of activity for shipping for many hundreds of years, so it is appropriate for this book to start by giving a run-down of a very special wreck that goes as far back as 1418, when it was built here during the reign of King Henry V. Classed as a clinker built Carrick, the *Grace Dieu* was around 1,400 tons and was actually one of the King's largest ships.

It is said to have only ever had one voyage: in 1420 the Earl of Devonshire was in command of a fleet of ships for a routine patrol, but on this voyage the crew mutinied and the ship was taken to St Helens on the Isle of Wight. That seems to be the end of the sea career of the *Grace Dieu*. The ship itself then spent the rest of its life in Southampton Water with a crew on board to keep it ship-shape, before later on being towed up the River Hamble where it stayed.

It was on 7 January 1439 that a lightning strike is said to have started a fire on board and the *Grace Dieu* was engulfed in flames until there was very little of the ship remaining. Anything useful was salvaged until the rest of it sank into the mud. Over the years parts of the wreck would stick out at low water prompting investigations in the 1800s whereby surveys were carried out to establish the history of the wreck and by then reidentify it. Measurements were taken in 1875 by a Mr F. Crawshay, which detailed the ship to be 130 feet in length, 40 feet in width and 12 feet deep, as well as finding out the more intricate details about the timber in which the ship was built from.

It would not be until 1933 during another investigation that it was identified as the *Grace Dieu*, this being confirmed by the National Maritime Museum over fifty years later during further work. As the years went by the wreck was visited by archaeologists and even had an episode of the popular TV series *Time Team* devoted to it, with excavations being carried out by them plus a team from nearby Southampton University.

What was more interesting as the surveys commenced is that nearby was another historic wreck that has recently been identified as another of Henry V's ships, the *Holigost*, roughly translated as Holy Ghost. It had been a captured Spanish vessel and refitted out for the English navy before being laid up here and slowly rotting away, anything around its upper decks being salvaged, broken and taken away over time.

Due to the significance of both ships, they are today sites restricted by the Protection of Wrecks Act 1973. *Grace Dieu* was listed one year after the Act came into force and now both this and *Holigost* are managed by governing body Historic England, who will oversee any future excavation and surveys.

2
Mary Rose

Possibly one of the most famous British ships in the world, the Tudor warship *Mary Rose* was built in Portsmouth in 1511 under the direction of King Henry VIII and named after his sister. It lasted almost thirty-five years and during that time it underwent a number of modifications that saw additional structure installed and a change in its weapons.

Under the command of Captain Roger Grenville, it was heading out of Portsmouth harbour on 19 July 1545 along with a fleet of the King's ships due to reports of a French fleet laying off the Isle of Wight. With the threat of an attack imminent the fleet sailed to defend the country, the King himself watching from nearby Southsea Castle on the coast. With around 500 personnel on board the *Mary Rose* was seen to turn to starboard as was normal when manoeuvring towards a battle position, but in this case the ship wasn't seeming to right itself.

Onboard the ship water had started flooding into the lower deck gun ports, preventing the ship from remaining upright. As more water came in the list to starboard increased until things started to shift from one side to the other and the weight distribution fell to a critical level. Guns and people all fell to one side and the ship heeled over much to the horror of the watching king and his men.

The *Mary Rose* as it was depicted in its heyday.

Tog Mor in position for the lifting of the *Mary Rose*. (Wendy Brown)

The *Mary Rose* had prepared for battle by installing anti-boarding nets all across the upper deck so that any potential visitors from the French fleet would find it hard to get on board, but this was what doomed the rest of the crew. The men below this netting were trapped and dragged down with the ship into the cold waters of the Solent and within minutes the entire ship had rolled over and sank. The only survivors of this disaster were those on the outside of the netting, mostly those people who took up position up the masts and rigging. There were just thirty-five people left alive.

Salvage attempts began immediately but all they succeeded in doing was breaking off the masts. After a long challenge with very little to show, the wreck was abandoned and left to its fate. It was not until 1836 that brothers John and Charles Deane were tasked with unsnagging some fishing nets that they realised that they had rediscovered the wreck of the *Mary Rose*. After almost three centuries the remains were considerably buried but they did manage to get several cannon raised (one of which is on display today in the Tower of London). After a while the enthusiasm dried up and the wreck was once again left to be forgotten.

It would be another century before anybody else took an interest and in this case it was historian and author Alexander McKee. He believed that there was something worth saving on this ship if only it could be found and so in 1965 he initiated a search that

Above: *Tog Mor* in position for the lifting of the *Mary Rose*. (Wendy Brown)

Left: *Mary Rose* dive team member Chris Dodds. (Michael Robertson)

would take him several years, using a small boat and members of the British Sub-Aqua Club (Southsea branch).

In 1968 an anomaly was found on the seabed but nothing could be confirmed until 1971 when finally there was evidence that the wreck they had located was in fact the missing Tudor warship. By now interest was growing in the ship and it was decided that a wreck of this importance should be raised, not just the artefacts but the entire vessel. For a job this big, they needed a lot of help and a lot of funds.

The Mary Rose Trust was formed and soon the likes of Margaret Rule became known, as the press now became interested in what was going on. Reports from the scene showed that the public were genuinely excited about this ship. With the plans being made public, the chequebooks started opening. People were only too eager to help once it became clear that the *Mary Rose* was going to be a huge deal. The plan was to raise the ship and have it on display in Portsmouth with all its artefacts preserved, catalogued and cleaned. This was a mammoth task, but not an impossible on.

Michael Robertson in dive gear
ready to dive the *Mary Rose* wreck.
(Michael Robertson)

Above: *Mary Rose* army dive team.
(Michael Robertson)

Left: *Mary Rose* cannon, Tower of London.
(Author)

The raising of the *Mary Rose*. (Michael Robertson)

Margaret Rule was not a diver, but she soon learned so that she could be involved in the project as much as possible. It was clear that many people felt rather pushed out when it came to the limelight, in many ways feeling it was not a team effort but a one-woman show, the man who actually founded the project and located the wreck being left behind. But internal conflicts aside, the *Mary Rose* was the one thing that kept them together, and the aim of salvaging an entire Tudor warship was going to be expensive. The Mary Rose Trust was going to need all the help it could get and with the objective needing teamwork, the personal grievances would just have to take a back seat.

Michael Robertson was a British Army soldier store man and in July 1981 he had just been told that he would be posted to 28 Amphibious Engineer Regiment, so he prepared to hand over to his relief. Suddenly one of the diving officers came into his office and asked if he wanted to become an army diver, to which he jumped at the chance.

After passing the course, Michael was pulled into his boss's office and asked if he wanted to volunteer to work on the wreck of the *Mary Rose* for a few weeks to assist in the salvage operation. The very next day he was on his way to Marchwood to conduct some training via the Royal Engineers Diving Establishment before being let loose on a historic shipwreck. By now it was June 1982 and training was well under way, their accommodation booked at the nearby barracks at HMS Nelson and off the army dive

Above: *Mary Rose* is on the surface. (Michael Robertson)

Left: *Mary Rose* raised. (Michael Robertson)

teams went in a civilian fishing boat to the support vessel *Sleipner*, a former Royal Navy ship now being used as the command platform for the divers.

From the rest of June until the end of July, the teams worked non-stop on the wreck of the Tudor warship, airlifting mud from the timbers and uncovering some incredible parts of the ship that had not been seen for over four centuries, with the visibility down to zero!

Being split into shifts, he was starting at around 0700 hours and while the work was fine it was very boring just hanging on to a shot line doing wet decompression, something that would not only prove monotonous but very cold to have to do. A decompression chamber on board was soon utilised. Owned by the Mary Rose Trust, this was very useful when being passed bacon sandwiches and hot tea through a hatch.

Above: People viewing the salvage cage holding the *Mary Rose*. (Glenluwin)

Right: *Mary Rose* in dry dock covered over now on display. (Christine Matthews CC BY-SA 2.0)

After months of only seeing a tiny part of the wreck, Michael was asked to carry out a survey of the entire shipwreck, which was a thrill to see from start to finish. The visibility was a lot better and there was a great view of what they had exactly been working on, the whole of the wreck now exposed ready for the lifting process to begin. Now the job they were asked to do was completely different – to start the construction of the lifting frame.

This was real engineering, putting the framework together, using jacks and strops while bolting sections onto each other, while another group of army divers were excavating a

Above: Museum is unveiled on 30 May 2013. (Author)

Below: The museum next to HMS *Victory*, 2013. (Author)

Mary Rose in its new museum, 2018. (Author)

tunnel actually under the hull using airlifts and water jets to blast the soft mud out of the way. During this period it was a great opportunity for trainee divers to have short period of time on the *Mary Rose* for the experience, the rest of the course being conducted back at Marchwood.

After many years of excavations around the wreck, the *Mary Rose* was now sitting on the seabed, the entire half of the ship that remained covered in what looked like scaffolding, parts bolted onto the actual wooden hull itself. The wreck was slowly raised clear of the seabed and dangled precariously while the cradle was placed underneath, before the wreck was gently lowered into the tailor-made frame.

Tog Mor was a huge floating crane, sent to Portsmouth especially to lift the wreck of the *Mary Rose*. The crane was brought to the scene and then connected up to what was now an entire frame bolted together with the warship wreck snugly fitted inside its protective cage. After several delays, the lifting process could commence.

It was 11 October 1982 and hundreds of small boats littered the Solent. Prince Charles had taken a keen interest in the salvage process from an early stage and was there to meet the army divers, as well as those who had made this huge archaeological excavation possible. With slow and careful consideration for the age and fragility of the wreck, the *Mary Rose* was raised to the surface, live on television.

'There is the wreck ... of the *Mary Rose* ... she has come to the surface!' the announcer told the watching cameras. Cheers rang out as the blackened timbers of Henry VIII's flagship saw sunlight for the first time in 437 years. But everybody watching held their breath as suddenly a leg of the frame failed and the wreck bounced in its cradle, the whole operation almost turning to disaster live across the world. But thankfully it was just a minor hitch that did not amount to anything, the wreck being fully exposed and placed on a barge ever so gently.

As the *Mary Rose* sailed back into its home port after so many years, the cheers and salutes ran wild. A dry dock was allocated for the huge task of preserving the hull, right next to Nelson's flagship HMS *Victory*. A temporary covering was erected and the hull was sprayed with water to stop it drying out.

Michael Robertson spent almost six months on the *Mary Rose* team and regards it today as not only a great experience but a privilege to have been involved. On 19 July 1984 an unknown sailor who had been found on the remains was interred in a tomb in Portsmouth Cathedral. By summer 1985 the ship was finally upright where it remains to this day, still in the same cradle that was used to raise it back in 1982.

Today, after a grant from the Heritage Lottery Fund, the new museum that surrounds the wreck of the *Mary Rose* attracts thousands of visitors a week, the hull being the centrepiece surrounded by three floors of incredible artefacts. Longbows, arrows, cannons, plates, jugs, games, bones from both people and a dog, cloth, ropes, cups and many other things tell us what life was like on a Tudor warship. Scientists are still examining many items today for what it can tell us about who served on board, their diet, their past times and their working conditions.

The children's TV show *Blue Peter* continued to report on the conservation of the wreck and often their presenters would be showing off artefacts from behind the scenes and even walking its fragile decks. Prince Charles (now King Charles III) is still President of the Mary Rose Trust to this day. Alexander McKee died in 1992, his legacy being the discovery and salvage that overshadowed his other books, the *Mary Rose* making him a household name. For all his work and effort, this book is dedicated to him.

In 2012 the author attended the official opening of the new museum, Margaret Rule being a guest of honour and the ships bell being brought in by sailors from the new Type 45 destroyer *HMS Duncan*, with much ceremony and fanfare. With the ship's timbers now dried out and the preservation complete, we can now look at our maritime history, which is so close we can actually smell the wood and be in the same room as Henry VIII's flagship, a ship that took so many lives but is today one of the most famous ships in the world.

3
HMS *Hazardous*

The Solent seems to be littered with wrecked warships, most of them British, and one of these that has come to light more in the last few decades is HMS *Hazardous*.

Originally a French warship named *Le Hazardeux*, it was built in 1698 and was fitted out as a fifty-gun third-rate ship of the line, 137 feet long and displacing 720 tons. Despite being built during a major financial constraint, it was a fine example of the design envied by both Dutch and English fleets. The ship was part of a fleet that supported the return of the Spanish treasure flotilla but thankfully was not present at the Vigo Bay disaster that sank the rest of the ships.

Le Hazardeux was loaned to a privateer in March 1703 and was escorting convoy ships across to Newfoundland in the July of that year, but did not have a future with the French for it came upon Admiral Sir Clowdsley Shovell and his fleet in the English Channel in 1703. It was soon captured and taken in tow and it was decided that it would be kept by the Royal Navy and used as a warship, keeping its name as close as possible to the original – HMS *Hazardous*.

It was commissioned into the Royal Navy on 27 March 1704 as a fourth-rate ship of the line and during this period had its guns increased to fifty-four and its displacement increased to 875 tons.

Unfortunately its time with the Royal Navy also did not last long, for it was on duty escorting merchant ships from America when it entered bad weather on the approach to the Channel off the Isle of Wight in November 1706. The convoy of around 200 ships struggled to take shelter from the storms and proceeded to the areas off St Helen's Roads on the eastern side of the island, but the *Hazardous* found itself aground on the sands of Bracklesham Bay where it was stuck fast.

The ship was clearly not going anywhere so salvage of the items on board began, as well as taking off the ship's stores. in less than a year it had been sold at auction. By now the ship was listed as having only ten crew on board. The lower decks were flooded and the ship was slowly settling into the mud of the seabed. Guns were taken off and reused and in the meantime Captain John Lowen was put on trial in a court martial held at Spithead where he was found guilty of the loss of his ship. This did not affect his career though and he later went on to command other ships after a brief reprimand.

By 1715 the final evidence of any kind of salvage of the *Hazardous* was recorded as a payment for a Captain John Cole on work done that year. As the years went by the ship sank slowly into the waters and scattered across the seabed.

The wreck was all but forgotten when it was finally discovered in 1966 where the discoverers raised a cannon but did not positively identify the wreck. Further divers making a survey of the area in 1977 located a number of cannon and timbers just 800 feet from the beach and only 7 meters down, research proving that this was indeed the remains of HMS *Hazardous*. The local divers who were now adopting this wreck formed the Warship Hazardous Prize Project Group (WHPPG) and went forward with an aim of recording and preserving the wreck site, eventually having it protected by the 1973 Protection of Wrecks Act.

Since then divers have returned many times to survey the artefacts and more recently (2022) a 3D computer model has been created so that people can sit at home and view the remains of the ship themselves and see a bird's-eye view of what the *Hazardous* looks like today.

4
HMS *Invincible*

The name *Invincible* is a word that conveys strength and resilience and it is one that the Royal Navy has always been proud of, for it has been the name of an aircraft carrier, battle cruiser and a number of other major fighting ships that for 300 years have all served the Royal Navy well, but the very first ship to be named *Invincible* is actually still here in the Solent today.

Originally a French warship, its name being *L'Invincible*, it was launched at Rochefort in 1744 and was a formidable fighting unit, boasting seventy-four guns spread out over two decks and a crew of around 700, a huge deal back in the 1700s!

It was on 14 May 1747 that the ship met it end with regards to its time with the French navy, during a routine escort duty taking a convoy to India. As the ship was passing Cape Finisterre off the Spanish coast it was stopped in its tracks by Admiral Anson and his fleet of fourteen vessels. The French and British fought each other until only two French vessels were able to escape. The rest were sunk or surrendered. One of those still afloat was *L'Invincible*, which was taken as a prize of war and recommissioned within the Royal Navy as HMS *Invincible*.

Its time with the Royal Navy lasted only eleven years, but in that time it became the flagship of no less than three admirals and deployed on several occasions across the Atlantic and took part in two wars with its former owners the French.

It was on 19 February 1758 that the ship sailed from Portsmouth under the command of Admiral Boscawen with an attempt to take the French fort at Louisbourg in Nova Scotia, but alas this was not to be for the *Invincible*.

It ran aground on Dean Sand in the Solent and despite attempts at salvaging the ship in one piece, it sustained irreparable damage before storms pushed the ship over and wrecked it. Salvage of the ship was limited to what could be plucked off the stricken ship; other than that it slowly sank into the seabed and was forgotten about.

It was in 1979 that a local fisherman named Arthur Mack was operating in the Solent and found that his nets had snagged on a seabed obstruction. After pulling away at it the nets were freed, but as he hauled them on board he found that he had caught something far more interesting than sea life – timbers from a shipwreck.

A team of divers were sent down to investigate and were amazed at the history that they had stumbled upon, so after some research they identified the wreck as that of the *Invincible* and together they formed The Invincible Committee (1758) in order to meticulously research and excavate the wreck. The remains came under protection of the 1973 Protection of Wrecks Act and today there have been many diving expeditions to learn about this ship and find out what life was like in eighteenth-century Royal Navy warships that were actually French built!

Above and below: Artefacts from HMS *Invincible*, 2011. (Royal Armouries, Fort Nelson)

With some people able to salvage items for their own personal keeping there have been many historic artefacts over the years end up for sale on internet auction sites, few people realising the significance of such a find and the history of the vessel. In the meantime further dives and excavations have taken place by archaeologists and those with the preservation of this relic at heart. A 3D model has been developed online for anybody to simply log on to Pascoe Archaeology's website and take a virtual tour of the wreck site. What remains above the seabed is now scattered over a wide area, various timbers and fittings sticking out from the mud, no doubt much more buried and awaiting the skills of the divers to finally reveal what lies beneath.

Today there are various artefacts on display that have been preserved from the wreck and much more recently an entire exhibition at the National Museum of the Royal Navy in Portsmouth dedicated to the life and times of the first *Invincible* warship. With much more of the wreck still down there, the story of this shipwreck is still being written.

5

HMS *Royal George*

One of the most tragic shipwrecks ever to occur and indeed the worst loss of life in a ship to date off the coast of Britain is that of the warship HMS *Royal George* at Spithead.

Launched in 1756, it was originally going to be named *Royal Anne* but the name was changed in honour of King George II and was launched as the *Royal George*. It had a career lasing twenty-four years, which included the war with France and joining the blockade at Quiberon and the French port of Brest before joining in with the fight against the Americans in the war for independence.

By the summer of 1782 it was quite an old ship and had seen its fair share of duties with the Royal Navy fleets. Its next mission was to relieve the fleet at Gibraltar; under the direction of Read-Admiral Richard Kempenfelt, they were to join the squadron under the command of Admiral Howe, but not before the ship was to have maintenance carried out while at anchor off the north-western corner of the Isle of Wight. On 29 August it was due to have work take place on a submerged cistern pipe and the only way for that pipe to be exposed was to have the weight of many of the items on board shifted to the opposite side in order to lean the vessel over slightly until the pipe was out of the water enough to be worked on.

The crew got to work moving stores and supplies, as well as the heavy guns across the deck, but it soon became apparent that water was starting to come in through the gun ports. The captain did attempt to correct the list but too much water was flooding in and very quickly the *Royal George* heeled over and sank where it stood.

Loss of the 'Royal George', John Christian Schetky, exhibited 1840. Presented by the Misses Trevenen, 1885. (Tate)

LOSS OF THE ROYAL GEORGE AT SPITHEAD. 1782

Loss of the Royal George at Spithead, 1782.

The sinking was so quick that hundreds of people could not get off the ship in time. The death toll is said to have been around 800 people, possibly even higher than that. On board at the time were not only the sailors but their wives too, knowing that this may be the last time they would see them before they sailed to the Mediterranean.

An inquiry concluded that it must have been the age of the ship that had caused part of the frame to give way, a verdict that sparked anger as all blame was shifted away from the senior officers. For over a decade the masts of the wreck were sticking out of the water and this was later the scene of the infamous 1797 Spithead mutiny, the remains of the ship a tragic backdrop for the sailors that demanded change.

As this area was an anchorage (and still is today), the wreck of the *Royal George* was a hazard to navigation and was eventually blown up by divers in the early 1800s, a salvage operation retrieving some of the more useful items first such as cannon and the bell. One salvage operation was conducted by the Deane brothers who had to interrupt their cannon recovery to investigate a new wreck, which turned out to be the *Mary Rose.*

Because of the number of salvage attempts and the fact that it was so close to land, the wreck of the *Royal George* has never been lost like the *Mary Rose* and *Invincible* were. Today it is a protected wreck, but parts of it that were raised are dotted around the country. One of the lions at the foot of Nelson's Column in London is made from melted down cannons from the wreck, another cannon is on display at Southsea Castle, and another in Fort Nelson on the hill overlooking Portsmouth. Further cannon were melted down to provide the base of Nelson's Column itself.

But the real legacy of the sinking of the *Royal George* is the fact that it still remains the worst sea disaster in British waters.

Richard Kempenfelt, captain of the *Royal George*.

Sinking of the Royal George.

Above: Another image of the sunken *Royal George*.

Right: Wreck of the *Royal George*.

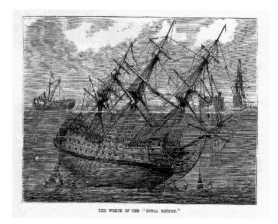

THE WRECK OF THE "ROYAL GEORGE."

Spithead, with the exact situation, and appearance of the "Royal George", wrecked with above 600 people on board — 29 August 1782.

Royal George still sunk despite salvage attempts.

To Colonel C.W. PASLEY, R.E., C.B. This Print representing the submarine EXPLOSION of the large Cylinder containing 2300 lb of Powder against the WRECK of H.M.S. ROYAL GEORGE, at SPITHEAD, Sep.t 23.rd 1839 — is most respectfully Dedicated by his obedient Servant

R.S. Thomas, Lieut.t R.N.

Published by A. Hinton, Portsmouth.

Print representing the submarine explosion of the large cylinder containing 2,300 lb of powder against the wreck of HMS *Royal George*, at Spithead, 23 September 1839.

Royal George cannon, Fort Nelson, 2011. (Author)

Right: Memorial plaque.

Below: *Royal George* memorial, Ryde. (MyPix image)

Nelson's Column at London's Trafalgar Square, the base of which was built using melted-down cannon from the *Royal George*. (Author)

6
HMS *Impetueux*

Another warship lost in the Solent area is that of the French naval vessel *L'Impetueux*, a seventy-four-gun Temeraire class ship which was launched in 1787. It served its country right up until the Battle of the Glorious First of June, 1794, the first and largest naval battle between the French and British during the French Revolutionary Wars.

As the ship fought the Royal Navy it became tangled up with the rigging of the warship HMS *Marlborough*, the ship already seriously damaged from gunfire. *L'Impetueux* was taking heavy casualties and after a third ship smashed into them both there was no going back. In the end the French ship and the *Marlborough* had both lost all their masts and their crews were in a bad state. Although the British ship could be towed away, *Impetueux* was too badly damaged and was soon taken over by the Royal Navy.

Now taken as a prize and renamed HMS *Impetueux*, it was taken to Portsmouth, but alas its time with the British did not last long, for on 24 August it caught fire and sank in the Solent having never been officially commissioned.

7
HMS *Boyne*

Another warship wreck in the Solent that came to a dramatic end was HMS *Boyne*. A second-rate ship-of-the-line, the *Boyne* had ninety-eight guns stretching along its 182-foot-long hull, the armament a mixture of 32 pounders, 18 pounders and 12 pounders, as well as ten 12 pounder guns forward and aft.

Launched from Woolwich Dockyard on 27 July 1790, it was commissioned the month after and with a normal crew of around 750, becoming the flagship of Vice Admiral Sir John Jervis and Lieutenant General Sir Charles Grey for their invasion of Guadeloupe in 1793. Despite a terrible time on board with an outbreak of yellow fever, the crew still managed to force a surrender from the French by April the year after with very few enemy personnel killed and no Royal Navy deaths.

It was two years later, on 1 May 1795, that the *Boyne* was anchored off Spithead in the middle of an exercise involving Royal Marines conducting practice firings when a

HMS *Boyne* on fire.

HMS *Boyne* on fire.

fire broke out in what is thought to be the Admiral's cabin. The evidence suggests that sparks from the gunnery drifted back on board the ship and started the fire. The crew realised very soon that there was very little that could be done and the flames could be seen for miles around, other boats heading to the burning *Boyne* to attempt to render assistance.

Also during this time it was necessary to move any ships away from the area to limit the danger of the fire spreading to other ships. What happened next must have been terrifying for the rescuers heading towards them – the guns began firing indiscriminately as the fire reached the loaded weapons. Two people were killed in this way alone, along with eleven others on the *Boyne* itself.

Very soon the fire reached the anchor cables and by 1400 hours that afternoon the flames parted the lines and slowly the ship began drifting across the Solent, the flaming wreck sailing past Portsmouth harbour much to the shock and horror of those watching from shore. At 1700 hours, as the *Boyne* touched the shore near Southsea Castle, a violent explosion ripped the ship apart and sank. The end of the ship had a dramatic effect on anybody involved in the rescue operation or those who were now coming to the shoreline to see the drama. The wreckage was thrown high into the air and rained down on to the people gathered and in the sea nearby. The career of this warship was well and truly over. By coincidence it had only been thirty-six years before that a similar magazine explosion had occurred at Southsea Castle itself that had cost the lives of seventeen people and ensured that ammunition was never stored in the castle again. How ironic that the *Boyne* drifting over to the castle would repeat history.

The remains of the *Boyne* were very prominent but over four decades passed before it was deemed necessary to clear the wreckage due to it being a hazard for navigation. On 30 August 1838 explosives were used to blow the wreckage up, although this was not entirely successful with a further attempt two years later.

The wreck today is marked by the Boyne Buoy. The ship is still there today but very little remains and lies at a depth of just 10 metres.

Thomas Elliott's *The Loss of the Boyne.*

8
HMS *Gladiator*

The Arrogant class cruiser HMS *Gladiator* was built at Portsmouth dockyard and launched on 18 December 1896, although it took another two years to be finally completed and wasn't commissioned until 1900. At 342 feet long it displaced 5,750 tons and was at the time of its sinking armed with ten 6-inch guns after a replacement from smaller weapons that were fitted from build.

Its first mission in 1900 was to the Australia Station, the naval post responsible for the waters around the continent as far away from Britain as you can get. But it was back in Britain that the *Gladiator* really made the headlines, making its way back into Spithead from Portland on 25 April 1908. The ship encountered terrible weather, the stormy conditions reducing visibility and making the crew push the ship to accelerate much faster than it should in order to retain the steering.

Nearby was the American ocean liner *Saint Paul*, who was also transiting the Solent at speed. Neither of the two ships could see each other until it was too late. When the bridge watch on board the two vessels saw each other suddenly appear out of the blizzard they

HMS *Gladiator*, 1896. (IWM Q 021285)

Ocean liner *St Paul* in 1895. (Library of Congress – Johnston, John S., photographer for the Detroit Publishing Company)

HMS *Gladiator* lies on its side after the collision, 1908.

HMS *Gladiator* salvage operation.

immediately reversed engines and changed course, but it was too late. The liner sliced its bow into the *Gladiator's* hull starboard side just aft of its engine room and water started flooding in.

As the *Saint Paul* slowly reversed, the warship was already listing with the considerable amount of water that was now flooding below decks, the hole in its side being too big to shore up so quickly. The liner stopped engines and lowered lifeboats to help rescue the hundreds of people who were now scrambling for safety in the icy water. Thankfully the crash happened very close to land and so the nearby Royal Engineers based at Fort Victoria swung into action and started to pull survivors out of the water and help them to safety.

In the meantime the *Gladiator* could not be saved and it settled into the shallow seabed on its side where it laid still, its hull resembling a beached whale with propellers. The entire disaster had taken just ten minutes. During that time twenty-seven of its crew had died; the bodies of some of its crew were buried in the Haslar Naval Cemetery nearby.

The *Saint Paul* had a damaged bow and so it limped into Southampton where repairs could be carried out, but *Gladiator* needed a full salvage operation and plans to raise the wreck started immediately.

The Liverpool Salvage Association started work on pulling the wreck upright within three months and the stage after that of patching up the hole involved strapping pontoons to the side of the wreck to steady it while it was carried out. Once that was completed pumps were started to eject the water from inside the hull until finally the battered wreck of the *Gladiator* was floating once again and was able to be towed into Portsmouth harbour on 3 November 1908, just over six months after the disaster. It was sold to a Dutch company and towed away the year after. A later naval court of inquiry blamed the *Saint Paul* but when the Admiralty sued the owners a high court turned the blame on to the *Gladiator*.

Ironically ten years almost to the day since the disaster, on 28 April 1918, the *Saint Paul* had been converted for war service and was being towed from a dry dock to a berth in New York without ballast when it capsized in the North River. It was salvaged the following September and after a long period of repairs was eventually put back to sea as a merchant liner.

Today the *Gladiator* disaster is commemorated at Fort Victoria where an exhibition tells the story of the heroic efforts by the rescuers to save lives in the moments after the sinking. At the site of the shipwreck, concrete base and bollards built for the salvage operation are still there today, the only evidence of a Royal Navy disaster that was so close to land yet cost so many lives. There is no memorial at the time of writing.

9

A1

Of all the submarines historically in the Royal Navy, the story of the *A1* deserves a lot more attention than it has received, partly because of its story and partly because it was the very first British-designed and British purpose-built submarine. Built in 1902 by Vickers in Barrow-in-Furness, it displaced 190 tons on the surface and was 103.25 feet long with a single propulsion system that gave a top speed of 11 and a half knots on the surface, 7 knots submerged. The lead submarine in its class, *A1* was a spin-off from the previous Holland submarines that had been built after much rejection from the Admiralty.

But tragedy struck the *A1* on 18 March 1904 when it was in the middle of an exercise in the Solent. It was due to simulate an attack on HMS *Juno* when the steamer *Berwick Castle* collided with its conning tower while on a voyage out of Southampton heading

A1 memorial, Haslar cemetery. (Author)

to Germany. This was not initially known about: a report by the liner that they may have struck something, possibly a practice torpedo, was not realised until the *A1* failed to resurface. The boat had quickly filled with water and the entire crew of eleven were killed, the sub coming to rest on the shallow seabed just 39 feet down.

An important lesson was learned that was soon implemented on future designs – a watertight hatch at the bottom of the conning tower. Within a month the sub was raised and brought back into service after repairs were carried out.

It carried on its service with the Royal Navy for several more years but was only ever taking part in trials, the whole submarine conception still very new not only to the Royal Navy but to the world. Its service lasted another six years until in August 1910 a build-up of gas ignited and the resulting explosion injured seven men.

A year later the submarine was taken out into the Solent and sunk as a target, where it was finally lost. It wouldn't be until 12 May 1989 that its wreck would be positively identified following a fisherman snagging nets on an obstruction on the seabed. Laying at around the same depth as it had sunk in the first time in 1904, the corroded wreck is intact, although surveys over the years have seen possible tampering by visiting divers. It was listed under the 1973 Protection of Wrecks Act in 1998 and is now under the care of Historic England.

In 2014 it was announced that the wreck of *A1* has become the first UK submarine dive trail and was open to tourists on strictly licenced only divers who can examine the sub with the use of an underwater guide, working closely with English Heritage and

Below left and below right: *A1* grave, Haslar cemetery. (Author)

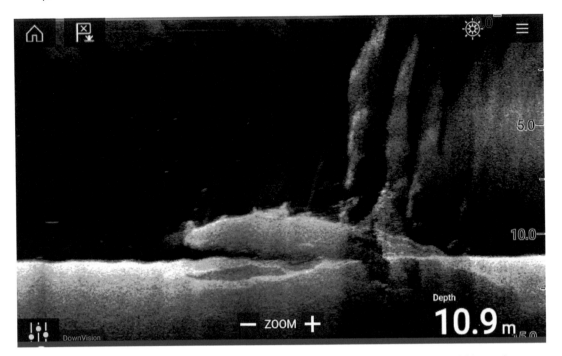

SONAR screenshot of HM Submarine *A1* showing the submarine profile and divers bubbles as they tour the wreck. (Southsea Sub-Aqua Club)

the Nautical Archaeology Society to make sure the wreck is enjoyed by divers while preserving the history of this unique and magnificent little vessel.

Today there are eleven *A1* graves that are tended at the Haslar Naval Cemetery in Gosport, bearing the names of the victims of the 1904 collision and sinking with *Berwick Castle*. The name of this submarine also appears on many other memorials. It was the first Royal Navy submarine to sink and therefore has unique significance in the history of the submarine service.

HMS *Velox*

Built on the River Tyne in 1902, HMS *Velox* was a new type of Torpedo Boat Destroyer that was powered by steam turbine, a revolutionary concept that had been tried on two other ships, the *Viper* and *Cobra*, but they had met with unfortunate endings and so the spotlight fell on the newly launched HMS *Python*, which was soon renamed *Velox* due to it maybe being considered bad luck to have a third warship named after a snake.

It was 215 feet in length with a displacement of around 400 tons, not hugely armed with just one gun (12-pounder) and five smaller 6-pounder guns, as well as two torpedo tubes. Its top speed was said to be up to 27 knots, although that was debated throughout its time at sea, and it had a crew of sixty-three.

Velox spent the next few years being tested and worked on to perfect the turbine for use within Royal Navy warships, bringing the ship up to a faster speed and better handling. However, it was not all plain sailing when these were being carried out and the ship met with a number of issues with the engines. The high fuel consumption together with the fact that it could not pick up a great amount of speed meant that it was not fit to be an active duty warship like the rest of the Royal Navy. An incident off Land's End left it adrift almost without power and propulsion, a dangerous situation that was thankfully soon

HMS *Velox*. (Photographer unknown)

HMS *Velox*, making 33.64 knots in the North Sea, September 1902. (Photo from *Page's Magazine* No. 6 from December 1902)

brought under control. Because of the difficulty in handling it, *Velox* was removed from its duties and reassigned as a training ship to be based at HMS Vernon in Portsmouth harbour (today that area is shopping centre Gunwharf Quays).

Under the command of Lieutenant Pattinson, the *Velox* was on patrol with HMS *Conflict* on the afternoon of 25 October 1915 when an issue with its condenser meant that it had to seek shelter in calmer waters in the eastern Solent to investigate the defect. But they never had the chance to sort out its problem, because suddenly two huge explosions rocked the ship, sending debris high into the air. With seriously injured sailors crawling all over the ship, Pattinson noticed that a large part of the stern had been completely blown away. Incredibly the *Velox* was still afloat and remained so long enough to get a tow line attached from the *Conflict*.

But the ship was too badly damaged to withstand the tow back into Portsmouth and it settled stern first not long after. The *Velox* disappeared from view around 1.5 miles from Bembridge, Isle of Wight. A later court of inquiry heard that the first explosion was a German mine laid by the submarine *UC-5* and the second blast was most likely one of the ship's depth charges going off after falling from the deck. Four of its crew were killed.

Today the wreck is very broken up, having been extensively salvaged over the last century, although a number of surveys in the 1970s showed that there were parts that were worth a dive and the *Velox* lays in two main sections. A number of artefacts recovered from the wreck are now in the Isle of Wight Shipwreck Museum and several other local exhibitions on display, with the wreck itself having been adopted under the Nautical Archaeology Society Adopt a Wreck scheme.

Ray Mabbs was one of the salvage divers who went on it in 1971. He described the wreck as laying in very shallow water, perhaps no more than 50 feet down, the wreck heavily smashed up with two bronze condensers on the seabed. His company salvaged the propeller from the wreck, one of several that it seemed to have – with four shafts

Above: Diver Ray Mabbs
model of HMS *Velox*, 2022.
(Author)

Right: Velox artefact owned
by diver Ray Mabbs, 2022.
(Author)

and a propeller on each! In his personal collection he has on display a model of the *Velox* along with a brass plate from a small arms magazine, the relics of a forgotten shipwreck, remembered by those few.

The Maritime Archaeology Trust today sponsors recovery and conservation of any artefacts and continues to survey the wreck for reasons of cultural importance.

11

Victims of the War – *Algerian* and *Luciston*

The war at sea in both world wars was a disaster for merchant shipping, the general cargo ship having to contend with mines, submarines, surface raiders and of course the usual peacetime disasters such as weather, groundings and collisions. So it is not too much of a shock to find that the Solent has its fair share of wartime sinkings.

One of these wartime victims was the steamship *Algerian*. Built in Sunderland as the *Flintshire* in 1896, it was 364 feet long and owned by the Ellerman Line. It departed its anchorage near Cowes, Isle of Wight, on a journey to Avonmouth in ballast at 0820 hours on 12 January 1916. It didn't get far when close to the Needles a huge explosion ripped into the hull on its starboard side and the ship began to flood down below.

The cause of the explosion was a mine, a common cause of shipwreck close to the main ports as German U-boats laid dozens of them hoping to get departing ships from all the major UK ports. The *Algerian* stopped in the water and was sinking fast. Its lifeboats were launched and thankfully all its crew escaped without a problem. But as the ship settled and the rate of the sinking slowed down, some of the crew along with its captain decided to re-board the *Algerian* and attempt to save the ship.

Several ships headed to the scene and the ship was soon taken in tow. By the early afternoon it looked like the ship would be able to get brought back to port, but not long after the inner bulkheads collapsed and the ship began to sink further. Attempts to beach the ship failed and it was abandoned for the last time. *Algerian*'s bow touched the seabed and the ship then settled over on to its port side, sinking in just a few minutes.

Due to the position of the wreck very few dives take place on it, the busy shipping lanes preventing expeditions from taking place safely. *Algerian* still stands up to 7 metres high in places but the remains are well broken up, although there is one boiler that is prominent.

⚬⚬⚬

With the threat of the mine ever present, it is never overlooked that the U-boats themselves were also close by and in the case of the steamship *Luciston* this was a direct hit by a torpedo. Built in Sunderland in 1890, it was 316 feet long and owned by the Luciston SS Co. Ltd. On the evening of Christmas Eve 1917 the vessel had sailed from Southampton heading to Boulogne in France with a cargo of government stores when suddenly an explosion stopped the ship in its tracks.

In an attempt to make it back to port, the *Luciston* headed to Southampton but only made it as far as the Calshot area, the ship running aground just over a mile from the castle. The vessel was now a complete wreck, the hole in its port side too bad to repair and no chance of refloating the ship back to sea. With the twenty-six crew evacuated it was left there to sink further, eventually being blown up over the years as part of clearance operations.

Today it is in around 16 metres of water and very flat on the seabed, although some of the engine parts can be seen if you are to dive it today with the highest point being around 4 metres tall.

The fates of the *Algerian* and *Luciston* show that being close to land meant nothing when it came to war, the U-boat menace showing that the submarines didn't even have to be there to sink ships when they could leave a mine and let nature take its course. Thankfully in both cases there were no fatalities and the wrecks today are quite close to each other within sight of Calshot Castle and, now over a century old, historic sites.

These are just two of the many shipwrecks that the Maritime Archaeology Trust has covered in its Forgotten Wrecks map, a project that aimed to record as many First World War casualties as possible on the south coast of England. Their hard work to help survey these ships and bring to light their stories is a fantastic achievement that will always be appreciated by historians and divers alike.

12
UB-21

The First World War was the first time in history that submarine warfare had become such a big thing. Unrestricted access to the world's oceans meant that German U-boats could sneak close to the British coastline and terrorise the shipping lanes by sending ship after ship to the bottom by the use of torpedoes and then disappear like it had never been there in the first place. The sinking of the Cunard liner *Lusitania* in 1915 brought it home to the world just how deadly a submarine could be against a surface ship and soon the U-boat became the biggest threat to the nation.

One of these U-boats was the *UB-21*, built at Blohm & Voss in Hamburg in 1915. It was commissioned the year after and soon found itself on patrol off the coast of Britain fighting a war that was already two years old. It was 118.5 feet long and displaced 263 tons on the surface (292 submerged), and alongside its twenty-three crew up to six torpedoes were crammed in, as well as ammunition for the single deck gun. It could dive to a maximum 160 feet, more than enough to attack and escape, and that is exactly what it did.

It was on 5 May 1916 that it came upon the Swedish ship *Harald* (275 tons), sending it to the bottom and claiming its first kill, but it did not stop there. *UB-21* went on to sink a total of thirty-three ships, damage one more and take a further four vessels as a prize of war. All these shipping victims of *UB-21* were in the North Sea off the Yorkshire coast. Not only that but on 19 July 1917 the submarine landed two men ashore at Robin Hood's Bay to commit acts of sabotage, but they were soon captured after getting lost. The submarine returned to the area on 4 September and opened fire on the town of Scarborough, killing three and injuring another five.

Incredibly the U-boat was never captured. Instead the end of the war saw it having to be surrendered at Harwich in November 1918. It was taken to Portsmouth where plans were drawn up to have it sunk for target practice and experiments.

So on 20 September 1920 the *UB-21* was towed out into the Solent and when the area was clear of obstructions, the Erebus class warship HMS *Terror* opened fire.

The submarine took hit after hit and photographs were taken for analysis showing the skin of the submarine blasted open and the metal of the conning tower peeled back like a cheap tin can. Eventually the submarine could take no more hits and it sank later that day.

The wreck was soon located and demolished the year after, making sure there were no snagging hazards. A sweep of the area confirmed it to be flat, but a survey in the 1950s found that the submarine was actually intact and sitting on the seabed 1.2 metres high. However, over time the wreck was surveyed many more times and the remains were slowly breaking up and scattering over a wide area.

Today the wreck is well broken up and mostly flat on the seabed, but there is a still a wealth of historic information and artefacts that can tell us so much about this First World War relic. Items from the wreck have been salvaged and preserved and placed in the Isle of Wight Shipwreck Museum. The depth of water is only 5 metres so easy to dive and explore, the position just three miles from Eastney Point.

13
V-44 and *V-82*

After the end of the First World War, a considerable number of German warships surrendered and were taken away by the Allies. Many would be scrapped, used as target practice or, in the case of the fleet at Scapa Flow, deliberately scuttled by their crews. Two ships that were languishing in Portsmouth harbour were the V-25 class torpedo boats numbered *V-44* and *V-82*.

The V-25 class was a style of large vessel consisting of seventy-one ships that were built for the Imperial German Navy, each one displacing 960 tons and were 277 feet 9 inches long, their armament consisting of three main guns of 3.46 inch and six torpedo tubes.

Upon the outbreak of war, *V-44* found herself under intense fire at the Battle of Jutland in 1916 whereby it launched two of its torpedoes at the British ships and the rest of its entourage followed suit. None of them hit the targets but a few of the boats were damaged in the return fire, although *V-44* escaped unscathed.

It continued serving on several campaigns of Channel raids and interference with the Allied fleets over the next two years including being in the Second Battle of Heligoland Bight, again surviving all of them unscathed in a war that saw so many ships go to the bottom.

Of the seventy-one ships in this class, thirty-two of them were sunk during the war, the rest of them scattered across the fleets and in many cases used as target practice, and

Portsmouth harbour wrecks of warships *V44* and *V83*. (Derek Fox)

Portsmouth harbour wrecks of warships *V44* and *V83*. (Derek Fox)

that is what happened to *V-44* and *V-82*. After being taken to Scapa Flow, these two ships survived the scuttling due to the intervention of British sailors saving them by running them aground, so while the rest of the fleet was now scrap metal on the Orkney seabed, the two boats were taken down to Portsmouth where they were towed out into the Solent and once again HMS *Terror* would open fire on the derelict ships.

V-82 was taken out on 13 October and later towed back into Portsmouth to be run aground onto the mud of the harbour. *V-44* went out on 8 December and was hit by several rounds before joining its sister ship on the mud. The two vessels were no longer seaworthy and were sold off for scrap in 1921, although nothing was done to dispose of the two wrecks.

They were sold again in 1927 to the Pounds yard nearby, who dismantled the two vessels partially over the next few years but over time they were slowly sinking into the mud and forgotten about.

In 2016, the Maritime Archaeology Trust came along and began to study the wrecks of the First World War in the south coast area and their researchers found that there was no record of these two vessels having been completely scrapped. Analysis of the area showed that the two ships were actually still there in the mud in between Whale Island and the modern ferry terminal. A check on overhead images showed that indeed there were man-made ship-like objects in the area buried in the mud. They were still there sticking out of the low water and nobody had noticed or knew the significance!

Paintings of the area during the time of the destroyers being aground give a great insight into what the scene was like after the two ships had been grounded. Further examination of the sources revealed that apart from *V-44* and *V-82* there may actually be more First World War relics buried within Portsmouth harbour. At the time of writing these two ships are being studied meticulously and at some point 3D computerised models will be made of the wrecks, bringing to light a truly forgotten piece of First World War maritime history.

14
LCT 427

Operation *Overlord*, also known as the D-Day landings, at Normandy on 6 June 1944, was the largest amphibious operation in history, involving over 15,000 troops, over 6,000 ships and 10,000 aircraft. With the headlines around the world making this dramatic and developing news story the priority, few would even know of a tragedy closer to home involving one of the landing craft.

LCT 427 (LCT = Landing Craft Tank) was returning to Portsmouth after an exhausting day of taking its cargo of Sherman tanks on to the French beaches with a crew of thirteen. The journey across the Channel was somewhat different to that of four years ago when bombs and terror befell any ship fleeing the German forces out of Dunkirk. Now the tide was turning and it would only be a matter of time before the Allies swept the Nazi's out of Europe for good. The craft was 192 feet long and displaced 640 tons. Its open decks were able to carry a vast amount of troops and, as shown in these last twenty-four hours, were a huge asset to the Normandy landings.

LCT 7074, a similar vessel to *LCT 427*, outside the D-Day Museum, Southsea. (Author)

The battleship HMS *Rodney*, which collided with *LCT 427* and sank it.

It was early morning of the following day, just after 0300 hours on 7 June, that the landing craft was slowly heading towards England again, rounding the Isle of Wight and making a beeline for Portsmouth. Nearby was the 33,730-ton Nelson class battleship HMS *Rodney*, a huge 710-foot-long ship that had been launched nineteen years previously and had gained a reputation as a formidable fighting force when it went after the *Bismarck* in 1941.

With a ship so large, a landing craft so small and the added darkness, as well as what must have been an exhausted crew on both ships after such a long few days on operations, it would have been inevitable that mistakes could happen. As part of a flotilla of landing craft heading back, *LCT 427* was suddenly smashed amidships by the bow of the Rodney, slicing the small craft clean in two and throwing its crew into the sea.

The chaos on board was over in minutes; the landing craft had no chance as the battleship steamed on. There was just one survivor pulled out of the water: twenty-two-year-old Able Seaman Kenneth Sumner. He didn't last long after his ordeal and died two days later. His fiancée, nineteen-year-old Margaret Hunter, only found out by a letter from his father telling of his death in service. She had last seen him in February and it would be many decades before she found out what actually happened to him. Like many of the families, they assumed their loved one was lost at D-Day on the coast of Normandy. Sumner was buried in the Naval Cemetery at Haslar in Gosport where it is today tended by the Commonwealth War Graves Commission. He is the only victim who has a grave – the rest were 'missing, presumed killed'.

For almost six decades the loss of this landing craft had been forgotten to history until in 2011 the Southsea Sub-Aqua Club positively identified the wreck. The two halves were laying at a depth of 32 metres in an area of restriction where the divers had to get special permission to dive by QHM Portsmouth and Southampton VTS. In the summer of that year a positive identification was finally achieved and the announcement of the discovery of *LCT 427* was announced by project leader Alison Mayor.

Above left: Diver Alison Mayer examining the Ready Use Locker, which contains magazines of 20 mm anti-aircraft ammunition. (Martin Davies/Southsea Sub-Aqua Club)

Above right: LCT 427 wreck near the bridge looking up towards the gun deck. (Southsea Sub-Aqua Club)

Right: Compass binnacle from *LCT 427* in Ray Mabbs' house. Today it is in the D-Day Museum. (Ray Mabbs)

Mrs Margaret Emmet, whose fiancé perished as a result of the sinking of *LCT 427*, lays a wreath over the wreck. (Martin Davies/Southsea Sub-Aqua Club)

Ray Mabbs is a diver who has spent many years in the Solent waters and has told the author of the time spent on the wreck of the lost craft. He had dived this unknown wreck in 1971, recovering several items such as the spare propeller, a gun and the compass binnacle. He talked of the open landing door at the bow being down on the seabed alone but close by, the two halves easy to swim around, the flying bridge being the main area of interest, which is the area where his salvage took place. The binnacle was shined up and restored, sitting in his living room for many years until he donated it to the D-Day Museum at Southsea seafront. Today it is on display along with photographs of several of those who were lost on board *LCT 427*.

15
The Flying Boats

At the very end of Southampton Water is the old Henry VIII fort, known as Calshot Castle, a place where today visitors can learn about the history of the buildings and the surrounding area, which is still festooned with huge aircraft hangars from days gone by when flying boats would operate from here.

In 1957 the Aquila Airlines plane 'City of Sydney' took off from here and got into difficulty moments later, crashing into a chalk cliff on the Isle of Wight killing forty-five people, at the time it was the second worst air disaster the UK had ever suffered. But this was not the first and it would not be the last time a flying boat would be lost in this area. There are numerous recorded incidents where these seaplanes were lost at sea just off Calshot, with three being lost very close to Calshot itself.

Built at Rochester in 1945, the Mk V Sunderland PP118 sank at its moorings in a storm on the night of 3 February 1950. Thankfully there were no lives lost when it sank. However, there was a near miss three weeks after when a fire broke out on board the raised wreck. Two mechanics were tasked with removing flares from the partly submerged wreck, which ignited accidentally, setting fire to the aircraft fuel and trapping them on board. RAF Leading Aircraftman Peter 'Andy' Anderson was working nearby and

RAF Calshot in 1946. (John Greenwood)

Flying boat *ML883*. (John Greenwood)

battled through the blaze to successfully recover them into his wooden tender. This act led to Peter being awarded the George Medal for bravery.

G-AGKY was built in 1943 as a Sunderland and converted to become part of the Aquila Airways fleet after the war. While attempting to take off during rough weather, it lost a wing float and was towed into the sheltered bay just north of Calshot where it turned turtle and sank. No lives were lost in this incident, with all five crew, twenty-six passengers and their luggage being removed before it sank on 28 January 1953.

The third aircraft lost in the area was Royal Canadian Airforce ML883, a Mk IIIa Sunderland based on Loch Erne in Ireland, that became a victim of a collision when it was struck at its moorings by a surface vessel on 17 December 1944. The aircraft was totally lost less than a year after being built.

In 2010, Calshot Divers (a local British Sub-Aqua Club branch) was carrying out some paper research on local wrecks and had been told about the rather unremarkable PP118 wreck. However, the chance recovery of a large propeller by the Calshot RNLI a few weeks later caused confusion – it was the wrong type of propeller for PP118. Suddenly the PP118 wreck site became a lot more interesting!

John Greenwood, the then training officer for Calshot Divers, managed to track down descendants of Peter Anderson and gain access to previously unseen photos and facts relating to the incident. One example was the photo of PP118 beached and on fire, which was in the Anderson family album. This photo was removed in order to get a better copy, and this revealed long forgotten handwritten notes on the back – one stating that

Above left: The grave of hero
Peter Anderson in Dibden.
(John Greenwood)

Above right: The propeller recovered
from the wreck by the RNLI,
now in the Solent Sky Museum,
Southampton. (Author)

Right: Another propellor still on the
wreck taken in 2010 during a dive.
(John Greenwood)

'5 minutes after this photo ... the engine fell off'. The wreck John and his team had been diving at Calshot still had four engines – it couldn't possibly be PP118. As part of this research, the son of Duncan Menzies, one of the rescued engineers, was also located and the two families met for the first time in over sixty years in 2014.

The fact that the recovered prop, and the three remaining on the wreck, are all undamaged would suggest the aircraft did not crash on take-off or landing. This leaves the identity of the aircraft wreck down to two possibilities. Later analysis of the paper records and an Aquila Airways staff reunion subsequently reveals that G-AGKY had been dragged up onto the beach and later scrapped. These are first-hand accounts of the end of PP118 and G-AGKY, meaning that the only aircraft still out there is probably ML883. With the wreck upside down on the silty seabed, the Solent double tides, and visibility so bad you can barely see anything. Positive identification is at the time of writing is still proving hard work.

With no tell-tale engine numbers yet found and still some research to be done, John and his team are 99 per cent certain of the identity of this aircraft. The three flying boats being lost so close to Calshot means that their stories have become entwined with each other, but finally their stories are being picked apart and told for the first time as the details of what happened gradually come to light. Calshot no longer has a flying boat base, the roar of four-engine, 25-ton aircraft the size of a Boeing 737 lifting off from the Solent has long gone, but the massive maintenance hangars are still there for all to see, now offering adventure training for those who like climbing, skiing, cycling and sailing.

But out of all three stories there is one person who shines brighter than others, and for hero Peter Anderson, he is buried in the nearby village of Dibden, his grave tended by family, a man who will now always be remembered for an act of bravery above and beyond.

16

Claude

This next wreck is strange due to the fact that it occurred in such a prominent location yet few people remember it. On Thursday 25 September 1969 the 1,244 tons Swedish gas tanker *Claude* sailed from Fawley refinery carrying a cargo of 895 tons of butadiene gas (an enriched butane gas which is highly explosive) and exited Southampton Water and into the Solent, cruising slowly off the Isle of Wight when a thick fog enveloped the area. It was owned by Transmarin A.B. of Sweden but charted by Gazocean Ltd of France to deliver its cargoes from Britain to the southern coast of France. Built by Jos L. Meyer Werft in Papenburg, Germany, in 1967, the Claude was 222 feet long and could reach a top speed of 12 knots on its single diesel engine.

With a pilot and fifteen crew on board, including Captain Elvin Fogelberg and his wife and young son, the ship slowly made its way out of Southampton Water and towards the Channel, but the thickness of the fog was making the ability to see any vessels very difficult.

Coming in the opposite direction was the 1,075-ton British Railways owned cargo vessel *Darlington*, which was inbound from the Channel Islands. Built in Port Glasgow in 1958, it was a single screw vessel owned by Associated Humber Lines Ltd operating out of Hull. At 232 feet long, it could reach a speed of just over 12 knots, its black hull plying the seas on a regular basis around the British Isles carrying a general cargo.

But today it too was finding the fog difficult to navigate, and just off the West Lepe Buoy at 0509 hours the *Darlington* and *Claude* saw each other, but it was too late. The cargo ship sliced into the starboard side of the gas tanker causing a deep gash and immediately the ship took on a list as water poured into it. Fearing an explosion, Captain Fogelberg ordered the ship to evacuate and a mayday was picked up by rescuers who soon had the survivors heading to Southampton and straight to hospital to be checked out. Only two of the crew and the pilot had minor injuries.

In the meantime the Red Funnel Line tug *Culver* managed to get a tow line on board and pulled the ship closer to shore, successfully getting the *Claude* out of the way of the shipping channels and grounding it between Cowes and Calshot where the ship could be steadied.

But in the meantime the *Claude* by now had taken on too much water and after flooding and taking on a heavy list it rolled over onto its starboard side just outside Southampton Water, leaving a huge salvage job to now undertake, the wreck positioned just off the shipping lanes with a large portion of the vessel still above water. With all survivors taken care of, the *Darlington* slowly made headway under its own power back into Southampton for repairs to its damaged bow, a job that would require it to head into dry dock before it was to leave port again. The crew of the *Claude* was taken to hotels after their situation was analysed and they had been checked out at the Royal South Hants Hospital.

A very small oil slick from the bunkers of the wrecked ship was dealt with by detergent as soon as it was seen, with the owners being contacted by the port agents in Southampton to let them know of the loss. The odd part of this story is that it barely made the national newspapers other than the odd small article, considering it was a highly explosive tanker wrecked in a busy shipping area.

Smit Rotterdam, the salvage experts, had spoken to the owners the same day to arrange recovery of the ship and its cargo, the job under the Lloyds Open Form, a No-Cure-No-Pay agreement that was standard for modern salvage operations. The first thing that had to be taken care of was the safety of the cargo. Special protective equipment for the teams was given out consisting of rubber protection suits, breathing masks and gas detection equipment with a safety officer supplied by Esso on an advisory capacity. On top of this there was a permanent motor launch despatched to keep an eye on the wreck by the Queen Harbour Master. A safety zone of 200 yards was put in place around the *Claude*.

With many meetings taking place between salvage teams, the Board of Trade, owners and the captain, there was a lot of planning now taking place. Two days after the collision the captain and his family were allowed to fly home to Sweden.

The salvage started straight away using the tugs *Barentz Zee* and *Maasbank* along with the salvage ship *Bever* and the sheerlegs *Condor*. Sheerlegs are floating cranes that can attach lines to a capsized vessel and with a huge amount of lifting power can slowly move a large vessel off the seabed and roll it back on to an even keel. As the sheerlegs were attached and the *Claude* slowly manoeuvred upright, on 2 October the entire operation was able to slowly move to the nearby small ships anchorage where the *Claude*, still

Opposite, above and overleaf: Salvage operation of the *Claude*. (Roger Thornton)

attached to the sheerlegs, was able to be worked on without having the issues with the weather that had started to slow down the salvage. A Portuguese flagged LPG vessel called *Cidla* was brought alongside the still-sunken wreck in order for the dangerous cargo to be transferred safely over. Amazingly it had taken just a week from the collision to the *Claude* now being upright and discharging its cargo under the watchful eye of the salvage teams and the patrol vessel.

The cargo transferring commenced on 5 October, almost two weeks after the sinking, the pumps working at 28 tons an hour, but during this operation it was discovered that one of the pipes had broken causing a leak of the liquid gas that threatened a massive explosion. The alarm was raised and outside authorities informed. *Cidla* was parted from the *Claude* and moved away for fear of explosion.

As soon as this leak was found, Captain Edward Kirton, Southampton's dock and harbourmaster, took charge of the situation and ordered the entire port closed down while emergency repairs were carried out. With the nearby Fawley refinery holding huge oil storage tanks the fear was that any blast would be catastrophic. The skills of the engineers working on the operation made sure that the port was reopened just after midnight the following morning, the *Claude* salvage operation commencing again soon after.

On 17 October the operation was deemed a success as the *Claude* was certified 'gas free' and towed up to Southampton where the ship was placed into dry dock for temporary repairs and an inspection to be carried out in order for it to be towed to Germany at the end of October 1969 for a full repair job to be carried out.

Thankfully the *Claude* never made headlines again. It was sold in 1974 to Antarctic Gas Inc of Panama and then went on to have a number of owners over the next few decades, as well as a host of name changes – *Caribgas 20* (1982), *White Star* (1988), *Eurogas One* (1988), and *Andrea Corsali* (1989). It was sold for scrap but rescued by a Chinese shipping company and renamed *Zhe Ping Ji 151* in 1993, being converted to a simple general cargo ship a year later. After that it was sold yet again and renamed *Andrae 1* (1995) before finally becoming the Belize registered *Hao Xia* in 1998.

It was deleted from the shipping register in November 2011 after there was no evidence that the ship even existed anymore. Where the former *Claude* went after its final name change is known only to a few.

As for the *Darlington*, it too underwent a number of name changes through the years. Two years after the collision it was sold to Sky Enterprises and became the *Gulf Sky*, later *Abadan* (1977) under new owners, *Petros P* the same year with same owners before being sold again in 1978 to Greek company Evia Sg Co. Ltd and becoming the *Ekaterini P*. In 1980 the ship had a cargo shift and developed a list soon after sailing from Rouen in France. It was taken into Brest where it was brought alongside and never sailed again, later being vandalised. Eventually it was towed out to sea by the French navy and sunk on 26 January 1982.

17
Pacific Glory

Of all the shipwrecks in the Solent area, the oil tanker *Pacific Glory* is one that hit the headlines more than any other, for this was not only a story of disaster, but one of skill, drama and, most of all, success despite overwhelming odds.

The 43,000-ton ship had departed Nigeria with a cargo of 70,000 tons of crude oil and after several weeks transiting the Atlantic it was finally reaching the south coast of England on the afternoon of 23 October 1970. Picking its pilot up in Brixham, the vessel slowly made its way east ready to head through the Dover Straits and on to its final destination of Rotterdam, a journey that the ship should have no problem undertaking.

Later that evening and into the night the *Pacific Glory* found itself parallel to another similar-sized tanker just a few miles away, the *Allegro*, with the lookouts on the bridge keeping an eye on them, as well as the traffic all around them. But as the night progressed the two ships started to come closer until around 2100 hours that night the two ships

The oil tanker *Pacific Glory* on fire after a collision and explosion, 1970. (Hampshire Firefighting Archives)

Pacific Glory after the fire was extinguished. (Hampshire Firefighting Archives)

came so close that their sterns touched when they both moved out of the way from each other at the same time. The *Pacific Glory* had a small amount of damage to its hull, its internal bulkheads letting a small amount of oil into the machinery spaces but nothing hugely serious. *Allegro* proceeded to go to anchor to check for damage but was deemed to be okay for now.

Incredibly the collision was not reported to the nearby shore authorities so when a huge explosion rocked the *Pacific Glory* two hours after the crash it came as a shock to all those who were now being told of this incident. Fumes from the oil had fed into the machinery and caused the motors to turn faster than normal and wouldn't shut down despite the crew's efforts. In the end a massive explosion ruptured the tanks and blew a huge hole in the starboard side of the ship, leaking burning oil on to the sea and killing several crew outright.

As distress calls were picked up, firefighting teams boarded tugs in Southampton and Portsmouth heading for the scene of the disaster on the south-western tip of the Isle of Wight, the ship now drifting towards the Solent very slowly. Lifeboats from the Isle of Wight, as well as three hovercraft, ferries, cargo ships, warships and aircraft now scoured the sea for survivors. A lifeboat from the tanker was found with several people on board, and more were pulled out of the sea suffering from burns and the ingestion of oil. The hovercraft were used to ferry the survivors to nearby Haslar Hospital in Gosport, which could transport them so much quicker than a regular ship and then bounce up on to the land when it arrived.

In the meantime the *Pacific Glory* was burning out of control. Fire teams took several hours to arrive on scene and then the choppy seas made boarding the stricken tanker that much more difficult. The ship itself was threatening the coastline if it was to break up so the decision was taken to force it aground so that as the stern settled onto the seabed it would mostly remain afloat and not drag the rest of the ship down. The plan worked; the fire was extinguished after a mammoth forty-four hours of hard work and the blackened hulk of the *Pacific Glory* was then handed over to the salvage teams from Smit.

The death toll was confusing due to the fact that the ship had taken on board a pilot. The press reported thirteen dead and twenty-nine survivors, but the truth was that there was actually fourteen dead (the papers calculated wrong – forty-two crew minus twenty-nine survivors meant thirteen dead without realising one of the survivors was not crew).

To salvage a ship on this scale took immense effort. First of all the oil had to be pumped out of the aft tanks in order to make the stern much lighter, a task that was easier said than done with the sea still being quite rough. The smaller tanker *Halia* was despatched from the Mersey to assist and after several attempts over the coming days they finally extracted enough oil to raise the *Pacific Glory* off the seabed.

During the fight to save and tow away the tanker, one of the tugs, the *Harry Sharman*, grounded at Culver Cliffs on the Isle of Wight close to where the stricken tanker was. On board there were barrels of chemical detergent and cleaning equipment. Now all that could be done was try and salvage what was on board as the tug had no chance of being refloated. The wreck of the *Harry Sharman* is still there today.

Pacific Glory as salvage operations near completion. (Roger Thornton)

One of three hovercraft that took part in the *Pacific Glory* rescue operation was *XW255*, now on display at the Hovercraft Museum, Lee-on-Solent. (Author, 2021)

With pumps running on board the tanker to get rid of excess water, the broken tanker was slowly towed away from Sandown Bay and taken to Lyme Bay where it provided a much more sheltered anchorage where the teams could be free to manoeuvre, as well as stay clear of shipping lanes.

Eventually the ship was brought back to a state where it could be safely towed through the English Channel to Rotterdam after a huge three-week operation from start to finish. On 14 November 1970 the burnt-out wreck of the *Pacific Glory* was towed away from the south coast of England and begin the final leg of its journey.

Eventually the ship was repaired and re-entered service, but another explosion in Hong Kong two years later killed two more workers. it was eventually scrapped in 1980.

When I first wrote about the *Pacific Glory* I asked many people if I could put a plaque up to remember the fourteen people who died. Unfortunately it got a negative response from many people in Southampton, Portsmouth and the Isle of Wight and so *When Tankers Collide* was published without securing a memorial.

But all that changed in 2021 when the Hovercraft Museum at Lee-on-Solent got in touch and told me that they had in their collection the actual hovercraft *XW255*, which was a Royal Navy hovercraft used for the rescue of the survivors of the *Pacific Glory*. Not only

Above and right: Unveiling of plaque on board *XW255*, November 2021. (Author)

To the memory of the 14 crew of the tanker *Pacific Glory*

Killed after a collision and fire off the Isle of Wight 23 October 1970 29 survivors were taken to safety and the fire extinguished thanks to the efforts of the hovercraft *XW255*, *SRN6-038* and *XT657*

that but they were more than happy to have a plaque displayed on board the craft so that it would be permanently on display on a craft that had actually been there at the time of the disaster. After securing funding from the Southampton Shipowners Association the go-ahead to place a plaque at the museum was given.

On 6 November 2021 the blue plaque commemorating this once forgotten disaster was unveiled by firefighter Chas McGill, who was one of the first on scene that night, and Brian Mansbridge, a former pilot of that class of hovercraft. Although we missed the fiftieth anniversary to commemorate the disaster, the fifty-first was just as poignant. Now at long last there is a memorial to those who died and those who fought the fire on the *Pacific Glory*.

18
SRN6-012

Another wreck that I have previously written about is the unique disaster that befell a hovercraft in 1972. Officially classed as an aircraft, the hovercraft was a new invention when the Portsmouth to Isle of Wight service was started and one of these early craft was the Saunders-Roe Nautical 6, abbreviated to SRN6, after the builders. Designed by Christopher Cockrill, the hovercraft was an incredible concept, a floating bus on an inflatable air bag powered by a huge fan that pushed it across the sea, gliding it at some terrific speeds and cutting journey times across the Solent to just a few minutes.

This class of hovercraft was proving popular with travellers and with a pilot in charge, the craft could easily carry over two dozen people from one side to the other in around seven minutes. There were several of these craft on the Southsea to Ryde route. One of them was hovercraft designated *SRN6-012* and on Saturday 4 March 1972 it was preparing to make the return crossing to Southsea like it had done several times that day.

The only issue the pilot had now was the extreme weather that had taken hold over the last few hours. Choppy seas and strong winds had caused a slight concern but not enough to warrant cancelling the service, after they had travelled before in worse conditions.

The early afternoon looked miserable with a cold wind blowing over the waters, *SRN6-012* set off with a total of twenty-six passengers on board, one of whom had noticed the windows and asked the question of how he would get out if there was an emergency. Somebody showed him how to break the window and he sat back in his chair, happy that his curiosity had been satisfied. Little did he know how prominent that comment would soon be.

SRN6-012 hovercraft capsizes. (Portsmouth News)

Salvage of the
SRN6-012 by RFA Swin.
(Hovercraft Museum)

SRN6-012 sped across the Solent with little effort, pilot Anthony Course aiming the bow towards the Southsea beach terminal near to Clarence Pier, slowing down as he brought it into the landing bay. Little did he know that the currents, tides and wind were now pushing his craft sideways just enough to cause disruption, the waves making the craft ride the peaks and troughs sideways on.

Suddenly the craft lurched to port as the side dipped down, but a gust of wind caught the slightly exposed starboard cushion and proceeded to actually lift the craft up out of the water. This got worse in the space of just a few seconds as the whole craft tipped up at a crazy angle and was very silently blown completely over onto the roof. The hovercraft was now upside down and twenty-seven people were now fighting for their lives underwater.

The passenger who had asked about the windows quickly put into practice what he had learned and smashed the window, others following suit and pulling themselves out of the cabin, swimming as best as they could to the surface just feet away. As the survivors' heads started appearing in the water the emergency services were already on their way after a nearby police officer radioed for help.

By the time fire teams had pulled up on Southsea seafront there were several people who had now made their way on top of the upturned craft, but they were slowly drifting back out to sea. A huge rescue operation was now under way with helicopters taking people off the craft and other aircraft landing on Southsea Common to ferry them quickly to hospital.

The craft soon sank, but not before all the survivors had been rescued. Firefighters tried to hack through the floor of the craft to get to the cabin to check for more survivors but eventually it went down. As the late evening newspapers announced the disaster, it soon became apparent that five people had died, one of whom would never been found.

The wreck of *SRN6-012* was salvaged soon after by the *RFA Swin*, a huge crane on the bow slowly bringing the craft up and taking it into Portsmouth harbour for investigators to examine. Incredibly the craft was repaired and ended up being put back into service in another country.

The inquiry established that the weather was to blame for the disaster, a freak accident that could not have been predicted and has never happened since. To this day the capsizing of *SRN6-012* remains the world's worst hovercraft disaster.

When I first wrote *Capsized in the Solent* in 2016 I did try and get a memorial up for the five who died but I was met with negative feelings about it. Also trying to locate survivors was a nightmare – most of them did not live anywhere near Portsmouth and were on day trips and holidays – and some weren't even living in Britain. The only two that I managed to trace were both long dead when I spoke to the relatives. But with the passing of the fiftieth anniversary in March 2022 a number of people came forward after finding out about the book.

Twenty-six-year-old Alex Kornfeld was an Australian who had only been in the UK for six weeks, working as a junior doctor at St Mary's Hospital in Portsmouth. He had done a few years of hospital work in his home country but wanted to travel and get further experience. As luck would have it there were opportunities available to train in hospitals in other countries and his doctor recommended Portsmouth as a place where he would thrive.

Still exploring his new country, Alex decided to go to the Isle of Wight and spend the day taking the bus around the island, despite the bad weather which he was still getting used to – a real culture shock for someone coming all the way from Down Under. Deciding to use the hovercraft, he carried no bags but his camera and ski jacket on top of his normal winter clothing that he would usually walk around the city in.

The crossing over to Ryde was a bumpy experience, so much so that he actually felt for his lifejacket, but after a few minutes of not being able to locate it he gave up, the craft coming to rest at the terminal. Although the ride was successful, he still felt uncomfortable. Putting his bumpy journey behind him he had a nice day out and spent the day as a tourist before heading back to the hovercraft, only just getting on board as they were closing the door. Taking his seat alone, the craft started up and began its journey across the Solent.

With the journey only lasting a few minutes, Alex noticed that this journey was very turbulent and found himself almost standing up in his seat at times before the hovercraft settled again. Suddenly there was a bang and the craft turned upside down, the reality sinking in as the *SRN6-012* settled on its roof.

'Oh my God this has actually happened!' he thought, as it suddenly became very dark very quickly. He realised that he was not injured and being alone he had landed OK, but those around him were making so much noise – the yelling and crying, mostly coming from the front end of the cabin. He couldn't make out anybody's face or have any kind of discussion but he knew that this was a very dangerous situation and he had to leave fast.

At first he decided to look for the lifejacket but water was flooding in from the windows that had been removed. He knew he was not a strong swimmer – a previous incident where he had been carried out to sea on a rip tide ended with him being rescued so he had been OK in the past, but this time he was in an upside-down hovercraft. In his head he realised that these craft were designed to float so he figured out that if he stayed where he was they should be all right. The craft was bobbing up and down but not sinking; fingers crossed he would be in an air pocket. If he was up top, he thought, he may be swept away by the seas or have to face the full force of the wind and cold.

Not being able to make out anybody other than noises, he knew that the craft moving backwards, forwards and sideways with the waves would soon flood further so he had to make the decision to leave the cabin. Clambering out of the window he came up by the side of the craft and saw someone else floating nearby, so he swam towards him.

'Do you mind if I join you?' he said, although he was not sure what he replied. With no context of how much time was passing he didn't know if things were happening fast or slowly, but he did think now that there was a good chance he could die if he didn't get something done quickly. He started to get a rising panic attack; as a medical student he knew that this was something he suffered from but this was very much stronger than before. He had a mixture of feelings all rolled into one – panic coupled with the fear and anger that he was going to die so close to land. He thought of all the effort and time he put into his career and doing a medical degree to have it all washed away in the Solent in a stupid accident.

Looking up, he couldn't see anybody else on the upturned craft and couldn't tell just how far or close it was to him. Then he made out one person stood on top of it, so he willed himself to fight the seas, treading water. 'If I get there I will survive, I will have a chance, otherwise I will die!' he told himself.

Someone reached down and grabbed him; he wasn't sure who but he now saw two people on the craft. He got up on top and reached back around and made out others in the water. He quickly worked with the other survivors to pull as many of them on board as possible, holding on to the skirt of the craft while others sat on his leg to prevent him from moving around while he was pulling survivors up.

What he did see that really upset him was the people being swept away far out, just heads floating alone, their image not staying very long before losing sight of them and knowing there was nothing they could do to go after them. Even as a doctor he still found it terrible, even though death was part of his job.

The pilot of the hovercraft stood up as the leader and he could tell just by his demeanour, calming the survivors and reassuring them, telling them that 'Help will come' to try make sure they had hope that their ordeal would not be lasting much longer. Everybody was weak and tired, unable to wave to those coming to rescue them as the boats were inbound from the harbour, as they had to hold on as best they could to the upside-down craft.

By now Alex was silent, caught up in his own thoughts awaiting rescue, broken by some of them singing 'Roll out the Barrel' and other songs to keep spirits up. He found this rather strange to see, but 'it made you realise how special it was to be a Brit'. The sense of calm now held everybody as a team: 'instead of being frightened, we knew that we were in this together'.

Soon the helicopters arrived, the pilot saying something about women and children first, something that became a legendary custom of the sea following the loss of HMS *Birkenhead* off the African coast over 100 years previously. The pilot was still knocking on the floor at a woman trapped under the hull, shouting to her not to worry, that help would be coming soon. Eventually the knocking stopped.

Like a miracle, a rescuer dropped by rope onto the craft and the rescue operation was in full force, the helicopters taking as many as they could before being stopped due to the torrential winds, boats taking over where they had left off. Alex was one of the last off the top of the craft, the boat taking him to the Royal Victoria Hospital in Portsmouth, a blanket draped around him. Physically he was well and he knew some of the doctors walking around the wards.

'Is everybody OK?' he asked one of them. But the sad reply told him everything about how lucky he had been.

'No, I've had a few bodies in here already. What are you doing here?'

He then went on to explain how he had ended up in the worst hovercraft disaster in history. As the months went by he did not go to the inquest. His time at St Mary's Hospital lasted until the end of the year, and he then moved on. The disaster affected him in many ways: sadness at the loss of the five lives but on the flip side it really made him appreciate the value of the human life, especially his own. Today he still lives his life to the full.

19
Flag Theofano

Although the Solent seems to be a major collection of mostly military vessels, the late twentieth century has seen a decline in the Royal Navy ships sinking here and more towards the merchant vessels. One of the most tragic of these shipwrecks is that of the *Flag Theofano.*

It was a stormy time in the Solent, the freezing weather making anyone caught in the wind and rain pull their coat around them tighter, if indeed they ventured out at all. But for sailors there is no let up from the surroundings that constantly bite at them, especially when the ship they are on requires work doing or evolutions carried out. It was on 29 January 1990 that the Greek cement carrier *Flag Theofano* was almost at the end of a voyage that had only started across the Channel at Le Havre, its crew of nineteen preparing to come alongside Southampton later that day while navigating a rough sea. It had been launched in 1970 as the *Boston Express* and went through a number of name changes through its career – *Ino A* (1971–74), *Rabat* (1974–80), *Victoria* (1980–May 1989) and finally *Flag Theofano*. Owned by the Golden Union Shipping Company of Piraeus,

Flag Theofano. (Photographer unknown)

Greece, it was 324 feet long and had a variety of nationalities on board – eleven Greeks, seven Moldavians and one man from Egypt – they would be under contract from Blue Circle, a cement maker, who chartered the *Flag Theofano* to carry their goods from port to port, in this case offloading what had been dropped into the holds via a large pipe in France and then had to sit around while the dusty cement settled enough to carry on the journey.

As the ship approached the Isle of Wight they made contact with Southampton VTS to let them know that they were inbound as scheduled and would be awaiting instructions to proceed. But in this case the ship would have to stay where they were. The pilot would not be coming out to them tonight due to the heavy seas so instead the ship was ordered to head to St Helens Road, an anchorage well known to mariners. They acknowledged the message and carried on as instructed.

At 1923 hours the *Flag Theofano* made its radio message giving its position and intentions for anchoring with the further plan to ride out the storm until the following morning. In the meantime the crew, led by forty-four-year-old Captain Ioannis Pittas, could sit tight until the morning. By 2000 hours that night a passing ship noticed it in the area. The seas by now were still choppy, with 60 miles per hour wind whipping up the seas, clearly no state for a pilot vessel to be travelling in.

By midnight Southampton VTS attempted to contact the ship but received no replies – not a big concern as many ships would leave the radio unattended if they were at anchor or vacate the bridge. A call for the nearby Bembridge lifeboat to search for a missing man was later found to be a false alarm and the boat returned to base. Otherwise it was a quiet, albeit stormy, night in the Solent.

Dawn the next morning saw the weather have no real improvements, but by now the arrangements for the *Flag Theofano* to come into port were set so they would allow the ship to proceed and pick up a pilot along the way. But when the pilot vessel made its way into the choppy Solent there was not a sign of the *Flag Theofano*. Figuring out that it may have weighed anchor and moved out they attempted once again to call it by radio. Again there was no response.

But it was later that day that the answers were found, a lifeboat bearing the ship's name along with two bodies and a life raft drifting ashore. It soon became apparent that the cargo ship had somehow sunk in the storm with not a single person realising, and it was too quick even for a distress call to be sent.

One man who remembers that night was Chris Bancroft, the coxswain on the pilot boat, who had been working the night shift. As dawn was breaking and the light of day was coming upon the still-stormy waters, he was asked by VTS to look for the ship somewhere near St Helen's Anchorage. 'Of course she was nowhere to be seen. We assumed that she had up anchor and (headed) out to sea. We went back to Ryde and I went home to bed. It wasn't till I switched the TV on later that day, that a lifeboat had washed up on Southsea beach and two bodies had been found.'

Knowing that nineteen crew were on board, even today Chris is upset by the loss of the *Flag Theofano*. 'Being an ex-seaman I felt for them,' he recalled over thirty years later.

The search and rescue operation was launched immediately with aircraft and ships looking out for survivors, wreckage or any clues as to what had happened.

In Memory of
Able Seaman Ibrahim Hussain
Tragically lost on the 29th January 1990
when the ship
'Flag Theofano' sank in The Solent
"Fair winds and following seas"
رياح منصفة و بحور متتالية

Above and opposite: Grave of *Flag Theofano* crewman Ibrahim Hussain. (Steve Hunt photos)

By mid-afternoon the wreck of the ship had been located – a number of bubbles were breaking the surface along with a piece of nondescript wreckage still holding on by a length of rope just floating on its own, a lone marker to a terrible tragedy.

It would be several days before the divers could finally catch a break in the weather and dive the wreckage of the ship, but by now any chance of finding survivors had long passed. There was always hope that they may be trapped in the wreck but there was no chance of getting them out in time if they were. Eventually a total of five bodies came ashore nearby, the rest still lie entombed in the upside-down wreck of the *Flag Theofano*. Four of them, including the captain, were sent back to their homes, but for Able Seaman Ibrahim Hussein, he occupied an unmarked grave in Kingston Cemetery in Portsmouth.

In 1991 the inquest into the deaths of the crew delivered a verdict of misadventure. An official inquiry report by the Marine Accident Investigation Branch the same year blamed a shift in the cement cargo in the storm as the sole cause of the disaster.

Today the wreck of the *Flag Theofano* is still there, marked by buoys to keep passing ships clear, now rusted and upside down on the bed of the Solent. Its propellor and rudder are the most prominent part of the wreck, the angle it rests at allowing divers to view underneath the hull to see some of the deck and superstructure. Diver Martin Woodward did a lot of work on this wreck to get answers for investigators. In 2022 he published a book on the story of the ship and his diving exploits on its remains. After I wrote a chapter on this shipwreck in *Britain's Lost Tragedies Uncovered* in 2020, I made several people aware of Hussain's grave being unmarked in the cemetery. Thanks to the generosity of the Southampton Shipowners Association, a headstone was designed and placed on his grave where a ceremony of dedication and unveiling was conducted in September 2022.

20
Dole America

Another cargo ship to meet grief in the Solent area is the *Dole America*, which, knowing the outcome of the story, seems to be more embarrassing than tragic. The refrigerated cargo ship was built in Gdansk, Poland, in 1994 and operated by Dole Fresh Fruit. It was 493 feet long with a gross tonnage of 10,584.

Dole America left the Caribbean island of Puerto Rico on 29 October 1999 and, despite experiencing rough seas during several days in the Atlantic, it arrived several hours late at Nab Tower to pick up the pilot. It arrived in Portsmouth harbour at 1800 hours on 6 November for the scheduled stop to discharge some cargo before heading for the next port of call at Antwerp in Belgium.

The following early morning *Dole America* sailed from Portsmouth at 0250 hours, the silent dockyard full of Royal Navy warships, their sentries on duty watching the cargo ship slowly sail past heading out past Round Tower and into the Solent.

Just before 0400 hours the pilot disembarked and the *Dole America* was now on its way to Antwerp with a crew of twenty-two from several nations, the nearby Nab Tower light visible on radar, as well as the light being visual. Nab Tower sits at the eastern end of the Solent and was placed here to help protect the area from submarine attacks during the First World War, the original plan having been for several of them to be dotted up the channel sporting guns and protective netting, but in the end only Nab was constructed and now served as a navigation point for passing ships.

At this point the bridge on board *Dole America* had some confusion about flashing lights nearby and they underestimated where they were, so much so that the ship collided with the tower at 0402 hours, just minutes after the pilot had disembarked. The ship bounced off the foundations and then struck a second time, causing damage to the ship.

The ship radioed for assistance as the crew now gathered to evacuate the vessel due to flood alarms giving an indication of water ingress below decks. As the ship started to list to starboard the pilot vessel turned back around and headed back to them.

With the Bembridge RNLI lifeboat despatched, the pilot guided the stricken ship and in less than an hour had run the ship aground to steady what was now a sinking wreck, while the nearby Portsmouth tug *Bustler* stood by to assist. These actions saved the ship from further damage and it was suggested later that the ship would have surely foundered if not for these quick actions.

The *Dole America* made headlines, not least the striking of a lighthouse so prominent causing ridicule from the media, the ship pictured listing and down by the bow stranded on the banks, its cargo of fruit in huge containers on the upper deck. After a week of carefully making sure the ship was structurally sound and that no further damage could be gained, three tugs slowly pulled its back into Portsmouth escorted by a police launch, where the damage was inspected. Three holes both above and below the water line were prominent including a huge gash in its starboard side, the visible signs of a collision on its hull. Over 5,000 tons of lubricating oil leaked into the sea. An inquiry into the cause of the accident blamed the actions of the captain and his lack of situational awareness.

The ship was eventually repaired and returned to service. At the time of writing it is still in service today, on much the same routes, under a Bahamas flag.

Above: The cargo ship *Dole America* in 2000, Portsmouth. (Photo by Andrew Thomas)

Left: The damaged *Dole America*. (Supplied to author)

21
Hoegh Osaka

Of all the wrecks in the Solent, one of the most remarkable ones of modern times is that of the car carrier *Hoegh Osaka*. Built in Japan and launched as the *Maersk Wind* in May 2000, the Singapore flagged vessel was renamed in 2011 and by 2015 was under the ownership of Hoegh Autocarriers. The huge vessel was bulky and tall, 590 feet long and 70 feet high, a crew of twenty-four operating it for the long journeys that were undertaken around the world with its cargo of brand new vehicles.

On 3 January 2015 it was loaded in the docks at Southampton with a combination of new buses, Range Rovers and a number of construction vehicles. The loading had only taken a day and by 1930 that evening the ship was ready to depart, its voyage commencing at just after 2000 hours. The *Hoegh Osaka* was on its way to its next destination, the German port of Hamburg.

By 2100 hours the ship was leaving Southampton Water and ready to make the turn at Calshot into the Solent on its way to the Channel, but several crew members were starting to notice that the ship did not feel right. The Calshot turn was conducted and the ship performed as expected, but in just a few minutes the entire situation changed.

Hoegh Osaka aground, 5 January 2015. (Author)

Hoegh Osaka aground, 5 January 2015. (Author)

The huge ship began heeling to starboard and would not return when orders were given to turn the opposite way. The ship had suddenly taken on a serious list and Southampton VTS was informed of the situation, but now the ship was heeling over so far that the propeller and rudder were clear of the water. The ship stopped engines and blacked out, the vessel now grounding on Bramble Bank at 2115 hours, the list to starboard now at around 40 degrees.

By now the sandbank had actually saved the ship for there was no doubt that if it had been in deep water there would have been no going back. A rescue operation had to be launched to rescue the crew who were unable to do anything for the ship. A helicopter began winching crew members from the upper deck while the nearby RNLI lifeboat rescued others in the water.

As the rush to get everybody off was underway, the first television images were breaking on the news channels as the *Hoegh Osaka* sat at a crazy angle on the sandbank. The following day crowds of people lined the front at Calshot watching the tugs attempt to move the ship and fail. News cameras gave live coverage as salvage experts pondered on what to do with it. So far they had an advantage of the ship not actually being sunk. Plans were drawn up to save the ship, but it would not be a quick process.

On 7 January the ship was gently refloated at high tide and slowly moved to the nearby anchorage where the ship was held in position by tugs, the bad weather a forefront of their problems but one that could be managed. Over the next two weeks the water that was inside the ship was pumped out and gradually the *Hoegh Osaka* was brought upright one degree at a time.

The progress of the salvage was covered on the news at each step, many people eager to see what was happening and how this mammoth task would be achieved, but on 22 January the ship was deemed safe enough and the tugs moved it back up to Southampton Water where it went alongside that night.

Above and below: *Hoegh Osaka* in Southampton unloading, 1 February 2015. (Author)

The cargo of vehicles from the *Hoegh Osaka* is unloaded in Southampton, 1 February 2015. (Author)

The cargo of new vehicles was a surprise when it was found that most of them were undamaged. Very few were lost despite the almost three weeks of being tilted over. After investigators checked the ship out and the few repairs were carried out to the damage, *Hoegh Osaka* sailed again on 10 February to have further repairs carried out in Falmouth.

An official investigation report blamed a number of issues for the near disaster, including the loading of the cargo, calculation of the ships stability and underestimating the weight of the cargo. There was no single person or incident that could be blamed for what happened. Today the ship is still working the seas. Hopefully lessons were learned not just for *Hoegh Osaka*, but for all owners of car carriers.

22

Solent Shipwrecks, Tragedies and Dive Sites

This book contains just a few of the dozens of wrecks and incidents that have occurred in this area, some of which made headlines, while others are forgotten. With the prime location for the Royal Navy at Portsmouth, it is not shocking that so many things happened in such a short time. Let's take, for example, the various mutinies that have plagued the ships: 1749 when the mutineers of HMS *Chesterfield* were executed, 1757 when Admiral Byng was shot on the upper deck of a ship for negligence, or the famous Spithead mutiny of 1797 when the sailors revolted against their officers due to the terrible conditions and pay.

There have been so many incidents, many of which have long been forgotten, such as the sinking of the *Claude* outside Southampton Water, the burning of HMS *Boyne* in 1795 and, if you go far enough around the Isle of Wight, you start to clock up a number of major disasters such as HMS *Eurydice* of 1878 or SS *Mendi* of 1917.

But just concentrating on the Solent area alone, for diver Ray Mabbs this has been a treasure trove of fascinating experiences and opportunities over the years. His company Spithead Marine Salvage were tasked to work on dozens of relics of the war, mostly things like propellers and precious metals that could be recycled. Many of the wrecks featured in this book have been visited by Ray and his team, such as *LCT 427*, from which he had brought up the binnacle that now resides in the D-Day Museum, or the brass portholes from a Motor Torpedo Boat that lies nearby in 100 feet of water. The list is endless. Three dive sites known as 'sausages' – round objects around 250 feet long that were used for the Normandy landings as booms – are dotted around the seabed in different places and nobody seems to have any idea how they got there!

HMS *Velox* was one shipwreck that was often visited by Ray, that and a similar ship, HMS *Boxer*, which was lost on the opposite side of the Wight. Both are memorable dives. Ray has a model of *Velox* and a brass plate from the wreck in his collection of mementoes. The physical items are a memorial on their own, but the memories of these dives will fade with time as the wrecks slowly deteriorate and are eventually consumed by the sea.

The locations of many wrecks are available for anybody who would like to pay them a visit via a copy of *Dive Wight and Hampshire*, a very good book that details the history of the wrecks, as well as the locations, and even points on shore where you can line-of-sight position your boat. With so much history littering the seabed it is the subject of many surveys by the Maritime Archaeology Trust, who has dug deep into the stories relating to the First World War shipwrecks. On several occasions there have been exhibitions at places such as Calshot Castle where artefacts from these remarkable ships have been put on display for the public to view and learn more about these forgotten pieces of maritime history.

There are many places in and around the Solent where the landlubber can search for evidence of shipwrecks and history in this busy and sometimes stormy sea. Haslar Naval Cemetery has the victims of the *A1* submarine disaster and the only body recovered from *LCT 427*, there are countless naval memorials along the seafront at Southsea, an entire Shipwreck Museum on the Isle of Wight run by diver Martin Woodward and not forgetting Portsmouth dockyard where the wreck of the *Mary Rose* is on display along with the *Warrior* and *Victory*.

The story of the Solent is one that is still being told. Many wrecks are still being uncovered and the memorials are only now being installed so many years after they had caused tragedy and heartache. The grave of one of the victims of the *Flag Theofano* is one that has now been given the memorial it deserves.

With two major ports having the Solent as their front gate, many hundreds of ships have sailed from here to be met with disaster at a later stage somewhere around the globe. The most famous, of course, is the *Titanic*, which sailed from Southampton on 10 April 1912 and was almost involved in a collision before the vessel even left port when a nearby ship, the SS *New York*, was pulled into the side of the great liner due to the immense suction of the two ships being so close. The quick-thinking tug master managed to avoid a major incident but just four days later the *Titanic* became the most famous shipwreck in history.

Same with Portsmouth, many warships setting sail past the famous Round Tower to be sunk in battle, the names being the subject of countless books, articles and even movies – HMS *Hood,* HMS *Royal Oak* and HMS *Affray* being some that are now forever engrained in our memories. These are the famous ones, but there are so many more incidents that temporarily occupy the evening news reports, such as the collision between the dredger *Donald Redford* with Hythe Pier up Southampton Water on 1 November 2003. There were no casualties but the pier was severely damaged and the landing area for boats and the train that ran to the end were disrupted for many months while repairs took place. A Marine Accident Investigation Branch report proved the captain to be at fault and he was later jailed.

This book is only a small handful of the most memorable lost ships; there are dozens more, ranging from warships to small tugboats and fishing vessels. It is incredible just how many ships can be lost in such a small area while being so close to land. This book could easily be doubled with information on these ships and the stories from the news reports from the time or the survivors who were almost taken down with them as they succumbed to the might of Mother Nature. It has always been my intention to help remember as many forgotten stories as possible through research and writing. There are so many more ships to write about, so many plaques we could put up to remember the victims and many more memorial ceremonies that can be organised. With the details of over twenty ships in this book and their stories told, let's hope that in the near future all the other wrecks will be remembered too.

Above: Maritime Archaeology Trust display, Southampton, in 2016. (Author)

Below: Forgotten Wrecks display, Calshot Castle, 2017. (Author)

Memorial overlooking Solent from Southsea seafront. (Author)

Above: Southsea Castle, 2011 – a place close to the sinking of the *Boyne* and *Mary Rose*. (Author)

Below: *Donald Redford*, Portsmouth, 18 October 2008. (Author)

Above and below: Damage to Hythe Pier after the *Donald Redford* collision. (Sath Naidoo)

Above: Anchor recovered from Solent. (Author)

Below: A wreck off the M275 motorway at Portsmouth. (Author)

Above: Wrecks litter the River Itchen, 2016. (Author)

Below: Ray Mabbs (far left) during a salvage operation. (Ray Mabbs)

Above: Ray Mabbs on one of his many salvage operations. (Ray Mabbs)

Below: Ray Mabbs' portholes from MTB wreck. (Author)

Bibliography

https://historicengland.org.uk – entries for *Grace Dieu, Holigost, Hazardous* and *A1*
www.maryrose.org

https://pascoe-archaeology.com/portfolio/the-hazardous/

Maritime Archaeology Trust – *Invincible, Velox,*
https://maritimearchaeologytrust.org/projects-research/hms-invincible-1758/
https://maritimearchaeologytrust.org/projects-research/hms-velox/

https://porttowns.port.ac.uk/the-sinking-of-hms-royal-george/

MAIB reports into the *Hoegh Osaka* and *Dole America*

Pritchard, Martin, and McDonald, Kendall, *Dive Wight and Hampshire*

Phillips, Ken, *Shipwrecks of the Isle of Wight*

Mew, Fred, *Back of the Wight*

Woodward, Martin, *The Forgotten Shipwreck: The Tragic Loss of the Flag Theofano and
Her 19 Crew in Solent Waters*

Acknowledgements

I would like to say a huge thanks to the following individuals:

Chris Bancroft
Wendy Brown
Alex Kornfeld
Michael Robertson
Ray Mabbs
John Greenwood
Roger Thornton
Sath Naidoo
Steve Hunt
Alison Mayer and the Southsea Sub-Aqua Club

And to those who helped who are not mentioned or wish to remain anonymous, thank you for all your assistance. This book wouldn't be what it was without people like you.

Also by Amberley Publishing

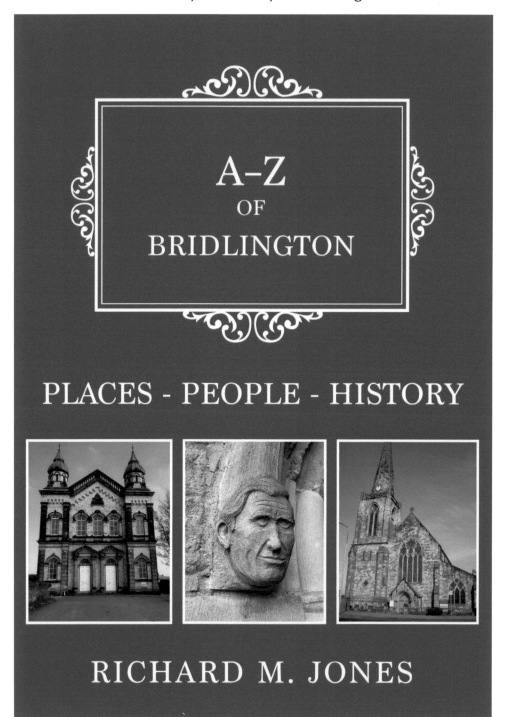

A–Z
OF
BRIDLINGTON

PLACES - PEOPLE - HISTORY

RICHARD M. JONES

ISBN 9781398117327